#BAKEITFORWARD

#BAKEIT FORWARD

recipes to bake kindness
and sprinkle joy

TRACY WILK

Photography by Alexandra Shytsman

This book is dedicated to all the COVID-19 frontline heroes. Hearing your stories gave me the courage to bake you a cookie when the world was crumbling.

In memory of my dad.
I promise to always honor your legacy
by baking all things chocolate.

CONTENTS

FOREWORD

by Zac Young

"Call me if the restaurant lights on fire." Those were my part-ing words as I left my new intern alone for her first solo din-ner service. A week before, 22-year-old Tracy had walked into the restaurant, her sparkling Converse sneakers the only sign of flair amid her buttoned-up, almost too ma-ture persona. She'd said she wanted to intern in pastry and was available on her nights off from her internship at ABC Kitchen. Interning seven days a week? This was the kind of cook I wanted to invest in.

With recipes and platings, Tracy was a quick study. By her second weekend, it was clear she had it down. It was also clear that she'd had it with me and preferred I not stand next to her all night, my face contorting with every move of her whisk.

That night, I had a date, an architect! Tracy flicked her hands and shooed me out the door, saying, "Don't worry, I got this." It was a gesture and statement that would be-come a routine interaction for us.

"Call me if the restaurant lights on fire," I said. I left for the date. After two cocktails, but before the food arrived, Tracy called.

I answered, then turned to the handsome architect across from me, "I'm so sorry," I said. "I have to go. One of our restaurants is on fire."

A boiler pilot light had sparked a blaze that gutted the

basement of the restaurant, climbing through the walls, smoking out the kitchen and dining room. No one was hurt, but everything below street level was incinerated, including Tracy's sparkling Converse sneakers.

The architect never called me again...but Tracy did.

Fiery yet loyal has been the hallmark of Tracy's and my relationship—the sparkly sneakers might be gone, but their spirit lingers.

A year and a half later, I'd moved to another restaurant group and needed a sous chef. I wanted someone who had drive, knew my style, and could take some heat. There was no need for a Craigslist ad, I knew whom I wanted.

You know that friend who can finish your sentences? Now imagine that in a culinary setting.

As Tracy moved up in the ranks from sous chef to pastry chef to executive pastry chef, our conversation morphed from my saying, "You know what this dish needs?" and her overlapping "sprinkles" to her waxing, "I want this to taste like" and my interjecting, "a McDonald's apple pie."

Our simpatico culinary viewpoints were impacted by a shared experience growing up with health nut parents. Naturally we rebelled by making the sweets of which we'd been deprived. It brought us joy. We were both aligned with the worldview driven by a "joy of baking" philosophy: Joy comes directly from our hands to our guests' experiences of our desserts.

Like soldiers in a foxhole, Tracy and I would peek around the kitchen door, to observe our (okay, *her*) S'mores Baked Alaska make its way to table 52. The diner's "oohs" over the flambé turned to giggles upon noticing the chocolate "twig" spearing the marshmallow-shaped dessert. We'd wait for their full-mouthed "oh, my God" to smile, high-five each other, and go plate another one. Like community theater performers who are paid by applause, our audience's glee was our preferred tender.

I saw Tracy pass this mentality on to our young cooks: Teaching them to perfectly emulsify a ganache, while sharing a mantra of delightful purpose to make the world sweeter. We aren't just making pie, we are making memories.

I knew Tracy would leave the nest someday and was fully prepared to make her plead her case for my approval and blessing. Seven years is a long time to spend with someone you aren't married to.

It happened. My phone rang. "Tracy Pastry" popped up on the screen. Her tab in my address book hasn't changed since Day One, only updated to include a picture of my dog posing with the ice cream pop squeaky toy she'd gifted him.

"I wanted to give you a heads-up," she started.

"Where are you going?" I didn't want to get needlessly emotional. I knew I could still keep her as my emergency contact.

"I'm going to teach."

I could hear her discomfort, caused by my uncharacteristic silence. I wasn't shocked, I wasn't sad, I was incredibly proud. I held out my silence only to make her squirm a little bit—after all, she was literally deserting me.

"Do it," I finally broke.

I was thrilled to imagine Tracy leading solidly technical, sugar-fueled lessons. The extra credit? A sprinkling of knowledge that the end result serves little purpose other than to lift spirits. Her journey to chef instructor had my full support.

In the shadow of a pandemic, leave it to Tracy to shine a rainbow light in the best and only way we know how. Those sparkly sneakers may be long gone, but their bright, glittering presence was already infused into the person who wore them. #BakeItForward is Tracy's mission of world betterment through baked goods.

INTRODUCTION

I started my baking journey as a child. I was originally drawn to the kitchen out of perpetual hunger. When I got older, I stayed there for the camaraderie it brought me. The kitchen makes me happy; it emits a sense of calm; it is where love is shown with a plate of freshly baked chocolate chip cookies. I suppose that's why I gravitated toward the kitchen at the height of the COVID-19 pandemic. I needed a safe space, and it seemed I was hungry for more than just food.

That hunger is what propelled #BakeItFoward. A grass-roots movement at its core, the idea came about when I realized we are stronger when we work together. I was in my home kitchen, and others were in theirs. We weren't together in the traditional sense, but being in the same conceptual space helped us share those feelings of joy, warmth, and love.

So I baked! I baked a lot, and when I couldn't eat it all, I shared it. I shared it with the postal service workers, the doctors and nurses, the firefighters, and the grocery store clerks. Making someone's day a little brighter, a little sweeter, is a way of life for me. A simple thank-you goes a long way, but I promise you, a batch of cookies goes even further.

I am so grateful to all of those who have opened doors for me (both physically and virtually!). Thank you for making me a part of your community. It is because of you that #BakeItForward has roots and continues to inspire.

The recipes in this cookbook are not meant to be intimidating or fussy. Many were influenced by my childhood, and I hope they conjure sweet memories of yours as well. I encourage you to share them with the ones you love and not take life too seriously. After all, there's nothing a little flour, sugar, and butter can't fix.

I hope this satisfies the hunger in all of us to connect. I hope that when life seems a little too much you'll remember that a lot can be solved with a warm cookie. In fact, it might be just what the doctor ordered.

BIRTH OF #BAKEITFORWARD

#BakeItForward was born of a desire to do something—anything—to combat the fear and anxiety of the early days of the COVID-19 crisis. When faced with challenges, I turn to my kitchen, and this situation was no exception. The act of sharing a cookie with my community opened doors I never realized were there.

The following stories, and the people behind them, are the backbone of #BakeItForward. I hope their words inspire you to continue to be kind, show gratitude, and give as much of yourself as these heroes have given throughout this complicated crisis.

A COMMUNITY OF KINDNESS

"During the onset of COVID-19, I was missing socialization and seeing my friends and family. I felt isolated. I enjoyed watching the #BakeItForward movement and was inspired. I contacted a friend who is a nurse and made the Oreo® Krispy Treats

from the #BakeItForward recipes and delivered them to a local hospital!"

"I saw the #BakeItForward movement and knew I wanted to be part of it! I was able to bake delicious treats for first responders, health-care workers, and grocery store employees. With lots of unknowns it's nice to be able to give back to the people who work so hard to keep us safe."

"I find that baking can be an escape and relaxation for me. And after gifting my baked goods, I bring a big smile to someone's face or make them happy. For a moment, they feel good and appreciated. This makes my day!"

"I have been telling everyone the story of #BakeItForward. You have inspired *me* to #BakeItForward, and I'm so happy my desserts can spread joy around my community!"

"It's truly amazing what baked goods can do to brighten the day of those who are dealing with this pandemic head-on. I made one delivery to a community behavioral health provider, who in one day had four clients die of COVID-19. I'm so grateful to have seen how happy they were when I dropped off the treats. It was a bright spot for them in an otherwise gloomy week."

A SPRINKLE OF HOPE

"We've got the miraculous people in this world who are going above and beyond to show the community how much they care—feeding the elderly daily, writing inspirational quotes

in our parking garage at work, donating supplies. These expressions of gratitude are what give me hope. Hope for a better tomorrow."

"I was riding my bike the other day, enjoying the beautiful weather, when all of a sudden I heard clapping and music. It was 7 o'clock, and everyone came out of their buildings and applauded health-care workers. I cried. They were clapping for me and the millions of other people sacrificing their lives to save others. It was a beautiful moment I don't think I'll ever forget. I'll be 80 and telling my grandchildren this story."

"I cry on my way home from work sometimes to de-stress. I ran into Tracy one day on my way home and she offered to make my unit baked goods."

"It was so sweet and comforting knowing people are doing everything to help. It's the little things in life."

"I love seeing the stories on the news about people recognizing those who are helping to keep us safe. Police, firefighters, health-care workers, grocery stores, pharmacies, postal workers, etc."

"The community's rallying together, showing health-care professionals/essential workers how much they are loved and appreciated is amazing. The world is seeing what careers/jobs are truly necessary when it comes to sustaining lives during a crisis—grocery store employees, pharmacy workers, truck drivers, post office staff, farmers—these people are just as exposed and still there serving the community. I'm thankful that their contribution to society is finally being recognized."

"I'm always inspired by how many people outside of health care have supported me and my coworkers. People from all different locations and health-care staff across multiple disciplines have come together with the sole purpose of continuing to provide quality patient care. During a time when everyone is socially distancing and patients are isolated, the hospital staff has rallied to put patients first, to continue to do what we were called to do."

"By far the most positive and uplifting time is every evening at 7 p.m., when NYC comes to together to cheer and applaud all of its essential workers! It fills my heart with pride to live in this wonderful city that rallies and unites in times of crisis like no other!"

"Getting a #BakeItForward drop-off made me smile when I most needed it. As a health-care worker, we are so invested in our patients and so focused on what is going on inside of those walls of the hospital. It was a nice way to step back from this nightmare and be reminded of the good people out there and the people who support us."

"We loved the #BakeItForward goodies! It made our day."

"It was a bright spot in an incredibly dark time. The cookies were delicious and appreciated by all."

"It was so thoughtful and made me so happy to see someone who doesn't know me or my colleagues go out of their way to make dozens of treats for us. I brought them in, and the entire ICU was overjoyed at how much dessert we had and couldn't get over how kind it was to see a pastry chef show us support."

"Tracy sent the most amazing goodies to the neonatal ICU. Her treats were the talk of the night instead of the usual COVID talk. Her generous gift made us feel supported, important, and so loved. I'm forever grateful for such a kind act."

"Tracy had reached out to us and offered a delivery of baked goods, directed specifically to the physical therapy department. Our staff have been working a shifted schedule since the pandemic began, working longer and later hours to accommodate the needs

"It was so thoughtful and made me feel so happy to see someone who doesn't know me or my colleagues go out of their way to make dozens of treats for us. I brought them in, and the entire ICU was overjoyed at how much dessert we had and couldn't get over how kind it was to see a pastry chef show us support."

of the patients and to decompress the crowded office. The delivery of baked goods came on a Saturday afternoon. The sweets, along with Tracy's heartwarming story behind them, helped boost morale and provided a moment for everyone to relax with a smile on their face."

THE PRICE OF THE PANDEMIC

"Nothing compares to the loneliness of being in a hospital room by yourself. If you ever felt lonely during your quarantine, remember at least you have a phone to talk to others, a TV to watch, and other distracting activities."

"My patients in the ICU, who aren't allowed to have visitors, are often too sedated or sick to realize what is going on. When they do open their eyes, all they see are monitors beeping around them, breathing tubes, wires, and the emptiness of the confined space. The only interactions my patients have are with their nurses. And we are like space aliens to them. We are in gowns, N95 masks, and shields, not even completely covered, but we don't let that stop us from giving the care to our patients that they deserve. I just hope my endless work, energy, and strength—including putting myself at risk more than 50 hours every week—makes a difference.

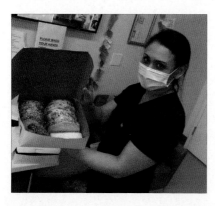

I hope in the end someone will look out for us and help protect us from all the physical and emotional damage we are facing daily. May God bless us all. Let us all be grateful to have people to come home to (virtually or not). Say 'I love you' often and remember those who do not have that opportunity."

"Yesterday I was mentally defeated. Silently observing the perfect little quarantine families with their perfect little schedules all over social media made me mad, jealous, and sad. I know I signed up for this when I got into health care, but did I ever imagine a quarantined world where thousands of people would fight for their lives alone in ICU beds, hospital hallways would empty, and nonessential health care would screech to a halt? No way. I go into work every day with the weight of 'What next?' upon me."

"I come home and I have nothing left for my family. I am mentally exhausted. I feel like I have aged 20 years. It is stressful, and my body feels it."

"I am unable to see my family, which is extremely difficult considering I am used to seeing my sisters almost every day and my parents on Long Island multiple times a month. I have not been able to see my friends, my cousins, my boyfriend. I have been living in a hotel around the corner from my hospital in order to keep others safe and not travel on public transportation and not expose people I live with."

"My mother cries daily because she knows that I work with only COVID-positive patients. I tell her that I love my job and that I can't see myself doing anything else."

"I am seeing things I never wished to see and being a part of something I never asked to be part of. I'm seeing more death than ever before. The lows are incredibly low, but the highs are even higher, especially when someone gets better. It's a roller coaster."

"Trying to care for patients while also worrying about myself and my health is mentally exhausting. It is very hard to detach."

"This has had positive and negative impacts on my mental health. I have never felt more isolated and unwanted in my life. Being a nurse, no one wants to be around you because you're 'dirty.' Although I understand their fear and believe it's valid to feel this way toward us, I can't help but feel so sad and alone going through all of this. We need people's support now more than ever. I will say that this has positively impacted me in regard to appreciating life more. It's given me time to reflect on what really matters and how the simplest things we've taken for granted are what we miss the most. I believe I'll come out of this a stronger nurse, daughter, sister, and friend."

"It has really been difficult to experience social isolation, especially as someone who is used to seeing their friends and family every day. I have a twin sister who is my other half and being away from her and my family for so long is what I find the most difficult. Not being able to control what my parents do in order to keep them safe; trying to get loved ones to listen and understand the severity of this pandemic; seeing friends traveling back and forth from Long Island to NYC, not social distancing, going to their jobs and then going back to their homes with their families is really frustrating."

"It is unnerving and unsettling going into work every day wondering if today is the day I will be infected. It is not just the exposure to patients that is worrisome; often it starts with my commute to and from work on public transportation. Then there are the days when we are notified that a coworker has just become sick. No matter where we look, the potential to be infected seems to stare us in the face."

CONNECTION IN THE CRISIS

"During this whole pandemic, our patients are alone. That has been the hardest part for me. They are scared, gasping for air, and are not able to have their family or loved ones by their side. On top of it all, everyone they encounter in their room is gowned up from head to toe and unrecognizable. I had a patient who primarily spoke Spanish, so communication was limited but she was anxious and I could tell she was nervous. I just stood there and held her hand for a few minutes and wiped her face with a warm cloth. I watched her slowly become a bit more comfortable, her work of breathing got better, and her heart rate slowly went back to normal. In that moment, I knew I was exactly where I needed to be. I may not have not spoken her native tongue, but I understood her."

"Patients die without family or friends by their bedside, but they don't die alone."

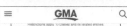

Wilk, who is a professional chef and instructor at the Institute of Culinary Education, saw the devastating effects of the pandemic first hand since she lives near New York University Medical Center.

INGREDIENTS, TOOLS, RECIPE BASICS, AND SKILLS

INGREDIENTS

Simply put, high-quality ingredients are the backbone of a successful day in the kitchen. It is so important to learn your ingredients and find the products that will help you create the dish you are the most proud of. These recipes were all baked in a small home kitchen, which I hope inspires you to keep a chef's kitchen at home.

FLOUR. Flour is of course one of the most important ingredients bakers use. I'll never forget how it was such a hot commodity during the height of the pandemic. However, keeping your pantry stocked with high-quality flour is something I always recommend. I prefer to use King Arthur brand, which publishes its gluten protein content, a valuable piece of information. The gluten content in your flour can change the chew and crumb of your pastry. I look for unbleached flour whenever possible.

- **All-purpose flour.** Used in almost all of the recipes on these pages. The protein content runs usually around 11%, which means we have enough protein to give our pastries strength but not too much chew.

- **Cake flour.** This has a lower-gluten protein, which is great in recipes like the Sugar Cookie Bites. If you can't find it, all-purpose will work just fine.
- **High-gluten flour.** This kind of flour is ideal for bread recipes, such as my Classic Yeast Doughnuts. Utilizing a higher gluten content, you will get more chew in your breads.

SUGAR. Whenever I teach my students about sugar, I always use the line "sugar is magic," because it is! I know we all know sugar as a sweetener, but it is so much more than that. Sugar can provide pastries their irresistible texture and flavor. It even helps provide rise. Almost all recipes will call for granulated sugar, but in addition to that you should have confectioners' (powdered) sugar, brown sugar, and raw turbinado sugar available. I love using Wholesome Sweet brand powdered sugar in my American Buttercream recipe because the tapioca starch flavor is much lighter on the palate than cornstarch, but any brand will do. For brown sugar I typically prefer light brown, but feel free to include dark brown if you prefer the deeper molasses flavor.

BUTTER. All of the recipes in this book call for unsalted butter. I always want to be in charge of my seasonings, and you can adjust the taste to your preference. European butter has higher fat content (and can be very delicious!), but as long as you are using unsalted butter you will be on the right track.

SALT. I keep two kinds of salt in my kitchen—kosher salt and a finishing salt. There is one salt I love to cook and bake with, and that's Diamond Crystal kosher salt. The grains are perfectly sized to dissolve in baked goods and large enough to pinch with your fingertips to season any dish. Feel free to experiment with different salts for your desired palate, but this is my go-to.

SPRINKLES. As the book's cover promises, sprinkles are a big part of my life, so of course I incorporated them into the #BakeItForward story. Keep in mind, although they are all important, not all sprinkles are created equal. Nonpareils are the small, round sprinkles, which I love for a garnish. The skinny stick variety is best for baking in a cake batter or cookie dough, as it will not dissolve as easily, therefore keeping its shape for a sprinkle-filled batter. I love Fancy Sprinkles for their high-quality look and taste, but feel free to experiment with different brands.

CHOCOLATE. When you work with pastries and baked goods, starting with high-quality ingredients is so important to get to the outcome of a fantastic dessert. I like to compare buying chocolate to a chef who is purchasing beef. If the chef purchases a lower-quality cut, she will not end up with a dry-aged rib eye. The same thought process applies to chocolate. The higher the quality, the better the result. I am passionate about bean-to-bar chocolate, a movement of craft chocolate that starts with the highest-quality beans, works to treat the farmers equitably, and transforms the cocoa beans into chocolate. My favorite brand of chocolate is Valrhona, which I have used in all the recipes in this book. Some recipes, such as the Mini Cookie Cakes, call for chocolate chips (in order to keep their morsel shape), but if not called for, chocolate couverture (higher-quality chocolate with cocoa butter) is used. You will see recommendations for caramelized white chocolate (used in the Potato Chip Cookies) and my favorite milk chocolate (used in Quarantine Banana Bread). For my standard bittersweet chocolate, I like to use Valrhona Guanaja, which is an even, balanced 70% dark chocolate. When I started baking during COVID-19, Valrhona sent me a generous donation of chocolate. If they weren't already my favorite chocolate company, their generosity solidified this choice.

LEAVENERS. There are three that I use in this cookbook: baking soda, baking powder, and yeast. Let me break it down for you. Baking soda needs an acid in order to activate, such as molasses or vinegar. Baking powder already contains that acid. Sometimes we use both in tandem, just to ensure we really get that rise we want. Yeast is what makes our breads fermented, fluffy, and delicious. I use instant yeast whenever I can, which allows me to use cold liquids and not worry about the temperature. This ingredient also allows me to control my rise time. You can use active dry, but just make sure your liquid has been gently heated up. If you prefer fresh yeast (which can be hard to find in standard grocery stores), simply multiply the amount by three—this is one reason why using a kitchen scale is helpful: 10 grams instant yeast = 10 grams active dry yeast = 30 grams fresh yeast.

VANILLA AND OTHER FLAVORINGS. I am a really big fan of using natural and pure flavors, which allow your baked goods to be bright and balanced. I love Nielsen-Massey Vanillas's vanilla extracts and flavors so much that I used them in the creation of this book. Their flavors are unparalleled with plump vanilla beans and other high-quality products. During my #BakeItForward work, Nielsen-Massey Vanillas generously sent me two quarts (64 ounces!) of vanilla extract, which lasted me just over a month. That's a lot of baking.

FOOD COLORING. While I like to keep my items as natural as I can, sometimes a dash of food coloring has its place. Gel food dye is essential to get the color you want.

TOOLS

Kitchen tools are crucial to getting desired outcomes. First and foremost, I try to always use a kitchen scale. When recipes go awry, errors in measurements are the most common culprit. We have tested all the recipes in both cups (volume measurement) and grams (weight measurement), but I would recommend using gram weight measurements whenever possible.

MEASURING CUPS are not created equal. Make sure you are using a dry measuring cup for flour, sugar, and other dry goods and a liquid measuring cup for water, milk, etc. If you are measuring a small amount (e.g., 1 gram), you may want to use a teaspoon versus a scale, unless you have a micro scale handy.

PARCHMENT PAPER is absolutely necessary, helping release your baked cookies as well as protecting your sheet trays so they last longer. I love using the lay-flat parchment paper to save me a headache, but it's not a necessity. If you are interested in a reusable option, nonstick baking mats are a great alternative and will last many years.

MISCELLANEOUS

A few other items I recommend are: a cookie scoop, to make evenly sized cookies; a pastry brush, to add shine with the power of egg wash; and a round cutter set. Rubber spatulas, whisks, and offset spatulas are essential.

DIFFICULTY RATING SCALE

These recipes are user-friendly. But since the basis of this book is to inspire you to bake with and for your community, refer to this scale to increase your baking knowledge and confidence.

1. **Gang's All Here:** Family Friendly
2. **Watches Food Network:** For the Home Cook
3. **Culinary School Groupie:** Advanced

- Mixer
- Rolling pin
- Cookie scoop
- Round cutters
- Pastry bags
- Pastry brush
- Offset spatulas
- Muffin tins, mini size and regular
- Food processor

Next to each recipe I have included any equipment that you may not always have on hand, so you can make sure you have everything you need before you jump in.

BASIC RECIPES AND SKILLS

SIMPLE SYRUP

On my first day of my internship at ABC Kitchen in 2010, I was asked to make a simple syrup. I was so nervous, you would have thought they'd asked me to perform brain surgery. Hopefully this recipe makes it a little bit easier. You can use this to glaze your babka on page 57, but it's also useful for cocktails, iced coffee, or adding a dash of moisture to your freshly baked cakes.

Active time: 5 minutes | Yield: Makes about 1½ cups

1 cup (240 grams) water

1 cup (220 grams) granulated sugar

1. Add water and sugar to a small saucepan. Bring mixture to a boil over medium heat. Whisk well to combine and dissolve sugar.

2. Once mixture is boiling, remove from heat and allow to cool to room temperature. Store in a covered container in the refrigerator for up to one week.

AMERICAN BUTTERCREAM

This recipe can be used as a base for any kind of frosting you will need. If wanted, you can reduce the sugar or add more to your liking. You can also flavor with any chocolate, taking care to melt it and allow it to cool to room temperature before adding it to the frosting.

Active time: 20 minutes | Yield: Makes about 1 pound of frosting (about 3 cups)

2 sticks/1 cup (227 grams) unsalted butter, room temperature

3 cups (360 grams) confectioners' sugar

1 tablespoon (12 grams) heavy cream

1 teaspoon (4 grams) vanilla extract

½ teaspoon (2 grams) kosher salt

1. Using an electric mixer fitted with a paddle attachment, beat butter until it becomes fluffy and just off-white in color.

2. Add confectioners' sugar and mix until well combined. Add heavy cream, vanilla extract, and salt. Mix until well combined. If using additional flavors, such as freeze-dried fruit or chocolate, add at the end, mixing until well combined.

3. Store in a covered container until ready to use. When ready, whip again with an electric mixer.

EVERYTHING BAGEL SEASONING

Although I credit Trader Joe's for popularizing this magical season- ing, if you can't find it you can make it easily at home. I prefer an unsalted version, so I can season per the need of the dish, but feel free to add some coarse sea salt if you'd like a salted version.

white sesame seeds

black poppy seeds

dried minced onion

dried minced garlic

1. Measure out equal parts of all ingredients (for example, 1 tablespoon white sesame seeds, 1 tablespoon black poppy seeds).

2. Place into a bowl and stir to combine. Store in a sealed container until ready to use.

PROOFING AND PREPARING BREAD

Not long into my baking journey, I fell deeply in love with the art of baking bread. I find it relaxing, a true form of meditation—but the act of sharing bread is even more worthy of sparking joy. As noted on page 15, I prefer instant yeasts, but the act of proofing and preparing bread just takes some practice. Your dough should go through three stages: first, the ferment stage, which will help the bread develop rise and flavor; second, the shaping stage, when the dough will be shaped and then needs to proof again; and third, the oven spring—when the dough bakes and reaches its potential, or full and final growth. Bake your bread to a mini- mum internal temperature of 190°F–200°F to confirm it is baked through, and make sure you allow it to rest before diving into it. Once you start baking bread, I hope you fall in love as well.

WINDOWPANE TEST

When you are making your bread, you want to knead your dough in order to develop gluten—or in plain terms, enhance and develop the chew in your final product. An easy way to see if your dough has been worked enough is known as the windowpane test. If your dough appears smooth and glossy, you are ready to check. Simply pinch off a small piece of dough (about 1 inch) and using floured fingertips, pull the dough between your pointer fingers and thumbs, stretching it into a thin windowpane. If the dough is thin enough to be able to see through once it is stretched without breaking, your gluten is sufficiently developed and you are ready to make bread. If the dough rips, knead for one to two minutes before trying again.

MELTING CHOCOLATE

Chocolate is a delicate ingredient, and it must be treated as such. Whenever you are melting chocolate, make sure to heat it over indirect heat. Since I don't have a microwave at home, I use a double boiler. I place a pot of water over medium heat, making sure the water does not go higher than about one-third of the way up the pot. Then I place a bowl over the pot (one that fits securely) and chop my chocolate into about $\frac{1}{2}$-inch chunks. I make sure I continuously stir the chocolate to allow it to evenly melt. But if you have access to a microwave, that is another great method: Begin with about 30 seconds, and then make sure you continuously stir to prevent burning. Once it begins to warm up and just starts to melt, you'll want to reduce it to about 10-second intervals. Continue until all of your chocolate is melted evenly, and enjoy!

Thank you NYU Langone PT Department!
White Chocolate and Macadamia Nut Brownies
Dark Chocolate and Walnut Brownies
Chocolate Covered Pretzels
Raspberry Rugelach

Todays #BakeItForward is dedicated to my Dad, who was an accomplished PT, marathon runner and Ironman finisher. These were my favorite desserts that I used to bake for him when I was a kid, and I hope these bring some joy to your day. I promise to honor is memory through baking, and I hope he is celebrated today.

It's hard out there right now for everyone.
And the world certainly feels a little crazy these days.
But through it all, you rise above.
Everyday you work, you put yourself at risk for the health and safety of others.
We could not be more grateful for the sacrifices you make and the risks you take each day. You don't complain, you don't slow down and you get it done.
Enjoy some sweet treats - it's the least we can do to say thanks.
We will continue to #bakeitforward to honor you and your families.

#bakeitforward is a grassroots effort to bring fresh baked joy (in the form of sweet treats) to front line hospital workers fighting the Covid-19 war. Join us! Chef Tracy Wilk bakes from her "sheltered at home"

Thank @cheftracywilk for providing us with these delicious cookies!

📍 BELLEVUE HOSPITAL CENTER

@cheftracywilk is using her #bakeitforward campaign to brighten healthcare workers days with baked goods! Check her out and support if you can!

sydcohen_

Thank you @cheftracywilk for making 17E smile!

NYC THANKS
EVERYDAY HEROES

GROCERS
PHARMACISTS
POLICE OFFICERS
FIRE FIGHTERS
PUBLIC TRANSPORTATION
SANITATION
CHILDCARE & TEACHERS
ANIMAL CARE
DELIVERY & COURIERS
& ALL OTHER ESSENTIAL WORKERS

heading to thank our healthcare workers now!

📍 NYU LANGONE HEALTH

iceculinary

This Pastry & Baking Arts student is making us proud 🍞

obsessedwithturtles

obsessedwithturtles #Bakeitforwad #wethankyou #healthcareheroes…

Swipe up to learn how you can join @cheftracywilk's #bakeitforward

movement!

COOKIES

CLASSIC SNICKERDOODLES

These cookies have become the story of #BakeItForward. In March 2020, the reality of the COVID-19 crisis began to hit home. Ambulances were getting louder, we were all under a stay-at-home order, and I was unemployed with no plan (and I always have a plan). So I did what I always do when times feel uncertain: I baked a batch of cookies.

This batch, let's call it the "first batch," went to a wonderful nurse named Sydney at NYU Langone. Sydney was a recent graduate who—like many of her colleagues near and far—was thrown headfirst into the chaos. And so it began. After that first batch, I baked nearly every day. My goal was to share and deliver a simple treat, to sprinkle my neighbors with a little joy in a dark time.

ACTIVE TIME: 45 minutes | **YIELD:** About 24 cookies

DIFFICULTY: 1 (mixer, cookie scoop)

COOKIE DOUGH

2¾ cups (330 grams) all-purpose flour

2 teaspoons (8 grams) baking powder

½ teaspoon (2 grams) kosher salt

1 teaspoon (4 grams) ground cinnamon

2 sticks/1 cup (227 grams) unsalted butter, room temperature

1 cup (220 grams) granulated sugar

½ cup (100 grams) light brown sugar

2 large (100 grams) eggs

1 teaspoon (4 grams) vanilla extract

CINNAMON SUGAR COATING

½ cup (110 grams) granulated sugar

1 teaspoon (4 grams) ground cinnamon

1. Preheat the oven to 350°F. Line two cookie trays with parchment paper, and set aside.

2. In a small bowl, whisk together all-purpose flour, baking powder, salt, and ground cinnamon. Set aside.

3. Using an electric mixer fitted with a paddle attachment, cream together butter, granulated sugar, and brown sugar. Mix on medium-high speed until the butter is fluffy and there are no lumps, about 4–6 minutes.

4. Once the ingredients are creamed, add the eggs one at a time, mixing until incorporated. Add vanilla extract, and mix until combined. Add dry ingredients, and mix until just combined.

5. In a small bowl, stir together the extra sugar and cinnamon for the coating.

(continued on next page)

6. Using a cookie scoop, portion the cookies and toss into the prepared cinnamon sugar. Place on the prepared trays, spacing the cookies at least 3 inches apart.

7. Bake 11–15 minutes, until just golden brown and centers are cooked through. Allow the cookies to cool for at least 5 minutes before removing from the sheet trays.

CHEF'S NOTE: Most snickerdoodle recipes call for cream of tartar (providing a slightly acidic tang, as well as a strong rise in conjunction with baking soda) but, in true "quarantine fashion," I had to make do with baking powder. After creating this recipe with baking powder, not only was I happy with the cookie, I had also eliminated the need for an extra item in my New York City kitchen!

SALTED CHOCOLATE CHUNK COOKIES

My favorite dessert is a chocolate chip cookie. I can eat one at any time of day, and they are the best way to tell someone you are thinking of them. These cookies are also the ultimate crowd-pleaser, so creating a great recipe for this book was super important to me. This recipe is perfect—crispy edges, gooey and chewy centers, and a little bit of salt. It's perfectly salty and perfectly sweet.

While this recipe is straightforward, following these two tips will make it over-the-top: first, use couverture chocolate instead of chocolate chips—couverture is chopped chocolate made with extra cocoa butter that melts and swirls throughout the cookie; second, be patient. If you're like me, the smell of warm cookies out of the oven is absolute heaven, but a longer resting time develops the flavor of the cookie dough. Allowing your dough to rest for 24 hours gives the dough a chance to hydrate. I promise it is worth the wait.

ACTIVE TIME: 45 minutes | YIELD: About 24 cookies

DIFFICULTY: 1 (mixer, cookie scoop)

---

2 cups (300 grams or 10 ounces) dark chocolate, such as Valrhona Guanaja 70%

2 cups (240 grams) all-purpose flour

1 teaspoon (4 grams) baking soda

½ teaspoon (2 grams) kosher salt

1½ sticks (¾ cup, 170 grams) unsalted butter, room temperature

½ cup (110 grams) granulated sugar

¾ cup (150 grams) light brown sugar

2 large (100 grams) eggs

1 teaspoon (4 grams) vanilla extract

Maldon sea salt (coarse sea salt), as needed for garnish

1. Chop chocolate into ¼-inch pieces using a sharp knife. Using a fine-mesh strainer, sift out any chocolate "dust."

2. In a small bowl, whisk together all-purpose flour, baking soda, and salt. Set aside.

3. Using an electric mixer fitted with a paddle attachment, cream together butter, granulated sugar, and brown sugar. Mix on medium-high speed until the butter is fluffy and there are no lumps, about 4–6 minutes.

4. Once the ingredients are creamed, add the eggs one at a time, mixing until incorporated. Add vanilla extract, and mix until combined.

(continued on page 29)

5. Add dry ingredients, and mix until just combined. Combine at a slow speed until about three-quarters of the way combined. Turn machine off, add chopped chocolate, and mix on slow speed until the mixture just comes together. Place cookie dough in the refrigerator for 24 hours, allowing dough to rest.

6. Preheat the oven to 350°F. Line two cookie trays with parchment paper, and set aside.

7. Portion the cookies using a ¾-ounce cookie scoop. Place on the prepared trays, spacing the cookies at least 3 inches apart. Sprinkle the top of each cookie with a pinch of Maldon sea salt.

8. Bake until cookies are golden brown, about 11–15 minutes. Let cool for at least 5 minutes, allowing the cookies to set up and finish baking before removing from the sheet trays.

CHEF'S NOTE: Sifting the chocolate "dust" allows the chocolate chunks to really shine through. Without this step, you will still have sandy bits of chocolate, instead of large chunks and swirls. If you want to minimize waste, save the chocolate dust for a cupcake garnish or to melt into your Chocolate Swirled Babka (on page 57).

GUAVA AND CHEESE RUGELACH

Throughout my childhood, rugelach was omnipresent. It was a must-have at our family holidays. This recipe merges my Jewish heritage with my Miami upbringing. Growing up in the Miami suburbs, we had a weekly Sunday barbecue. We'd shop for fresh produce at our local market, Norman Brothers. Included in our cart of fresh fish, produce, and other health foods was always a pint of rugelach for dessert. We'd all usually eat one or two pieces, leaving one piece left—whoever got to the last piece first was able to enjoy the last treat for the week. In this recipe, I pay homage to my Miami roots with a play on the iconic Cuban Pastelitos de guayaba y queso.

ACTIVE TIME: 45 minutes | DOWN TIME: 60 minutes

YIELD: About 24 cookies | DIFFICULTY: 2 (mixer, rolling pin)

COOKIE DOUGH

1 stick, ½ cup (113 grams) unsalted butter, room temperature

1 block (226 grams or 8 ounces) cream cheese, room temperature

⅓ cup (70 grams) granulated sugar

1 teaspoon (4 grams) kosher salt

4 large (80 grams) egg yolks

2 teaspoons (8 grams) vanilla extract

2½ cups (300 grams) all-purpose flour

FILLING

½ block (113 grams or 4 ounces) cream cheese, softened to room temperature

½ cup (113 grams or 4 ounces) guava paste, ¼-inch pieces

RUGELACH ASSEMBLY

1 large egg mixed with 1 teaspoon water (for egg wash)

Granulated sugar, as needed, to sprinkle on top

1. Preheat the oven to 350°F. Line two cookie trays with parchment paper and set aside.

2. Using an electric mixer fitted with a paddle attachment on medium speed, cream together the butter, cream cheese, sugar, and salt until light and fluffy, about 8 minutes.

3. Add the egg yolks and vanilla, and mix until combined. Add the flour, and mix until just combined.

4. Remove the dough and divide into 2 equal parts and wrap in plastic wrap, shaping the dough into a round disk. Allow dough to chill in the fridge for 1 hour.

5. Remove one piece of dough from the fridge. Using a lightly floured surface, roll each piece of dough into a 10-inch circle, about ¼ inch thick. Using a small offset spatula, spread cream cheese thinly on the dough, leaving a ¼-inch margin

(continued on next page)

around the edge. Clean off the spatula, and follow with the guava paste.

6. With a sharp knife, divide the dough into 8 equal wedges. Starting with the widest edge, roll the dough into a crescent shape. Repeat with remaining dough.

7. Place on the prepared trays, spacing the cookies about 1 inch apart. Whisk together egg and water. To finish, lightly brush egg wash on top of each cookie and sprinkle with additional sugar.

8. Bake cookies until golden brown and flaky, about 20–25 minutes.

CHEF'S NOTE: For this nontraditional version of rugelach, you want to make sure your cream cheese is truly softened. This will allow you to spread the cream cheese around the dough round. The guava paste will melt in the oven, but taking that step of cutting the guava into small pieces will help you cover the round evenly.

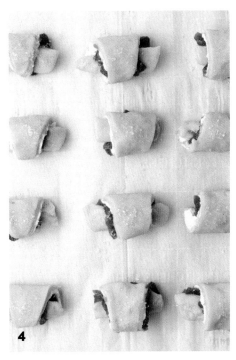

OLD-FASHIONED OATMEAL CREAM PIES

Although you can use this cookie base for a tasty oatmeal cookie, sandwiching these cookies with vanilla frosting may bring you right back to Little Debbie® Oatmeal Creme Pies.

ACTIVE TIME: 60 minutes | YIELD: About 12 sandwich cookies
DIFFICULTY: 2 (mixer, cookie scoop, round cutters, pastry bag)

COOKIES

1 cup (100 grams) old-fashioned oats

²/₃ cup (80 grams) all-purpose flour

½ teaspoon (2 grams) baking soda

¼ teaspoon (2 grams) ground cinnamon

¼ teaspoon (1 gram) kosher salt

1 stick/½ cup (113 grams) unsalted butter, room temperature

¹/₃ cup (70 grams) granulated sugar

2 tablespoons (24 grams) light brown sugar

1 large (50 grams) egg

½ teaspoon (2 grams) vanilla extract

FROSTING

2 sticks/1 cup (227 grams) unsalted butter, room temperature

3 cups (360 grams) confectioners' sugar

1 tablespoon (12 grams) heavy cream

1 teaspoon (4 grams) vanilla extract

½ teaspoon (2 grams) kosher salt

1. Preheat the oven to 350°F. Line two cookie trays with parchment paper and set aside.

2. In a medium bowl, combine the oats, flour, baking soda, ground cinnamon, and salt. Whisk together and set aside.

3. Using an electric mixer fitted with a paddle attachment, cream together butter, sugar, and light brown sugar on medium speed until butter is light.

4. Once the butter and sugar are creamed, turn speed to low. Add egg and vanilla. Mix for about 30 seconds, just until combined.

5. Stop the mixer and add dry ingredients. Mix on slow speed until just combined.

6. Portion the cookies using a ¾-ounce cookie scoop. Place on the prepared trays, spacing the cookies about 3 inches apart.

7. Bake until cookies are golden brown, about 10–12 minutes. Allow to cool for at least 5 minutes before removing from the sheet tray.

(continued on next page)

ASSEMBLY

1. Using a biscuit cutter or a round cookie cutter, punch out cookie rounds in order to shape the cookies into perfect rounds (optional).

2. Match up similar sized cookie rounds, pairing cookies together. Set aside and prepare frosting.

3. Using an electric mixer fitted with a paddle attachment, beat butter until it becomes fluffy and just off-white in color.

4. Add confectioners' sugar, and mix until well combined. Add heavy cream, vanilla extract, and salt. Mix until well combined.

5. Place frosting in a pastry bag. Flip cookies over and pipe frosting in the center of one cookie from each pair. Top with remaining cookies, creating a cookie sandwich. Place cookies in the refrigerator for about 1 hour, allowing the filling to firm up.

> **CHEF'S NOTE:** I like to use a round cookie cutter to shape these cookies after they are baked into perfect circles, but if you're ready to get to the filling part, feel free to omit this step. I recommend filling the cookies and then letting them firm up in the fridge before serving, allowing the filling to stay put, but if you can't resist, I understand!

VANILLA BEAN SHORTBREAD

These shortbread cookies are buttery treats that go well with tea or crème brûlée or as an afternoon snack. But don't just think of them as a treat for the vanilla lovers in your life. If you are looking for another flavor option, you can swap out the vanilla bean for a few teaspoons of a winter spice blend (e.g., cinnamon, nutmeg, cardamom), or add fresh lemon or lime zest for a citrus twist. Think of this shortbread as a base, and you can transform this cookie dough to highlight whichever flavors you love most.

ACTIVE TIME: 45 minutes | **DOWN TIME:** 30 minutes

YIELD: Makes 20 cookies | **DIFFICULTY:** 1 (mixer, pastry brush, food processor)

---

1 stick/½ cup plus 2 tablespoons (145 grams) unsalted butter, room temperature

¼ cup (55 grams) granulated sugar

1 vanilla bean, seeds scraped, pod reserved

½ teaspoon (2 grams) kosher salt

1 teaspoon (4 grams) vanilla extract

1²/₃ cups (200 grams) all-purpose flour

¼ cup (60 grams) raw turbinado sugar

1 egg mixed with 1 teaspoon water (for egg wash)

1. Using a stand mixer fitted with a paddle attachment, cream together the butter, granulated sugar, and vanilla bean seeds. Mix on medium speed until the butter is fluffy. This will take about 10 minutes, depending on the temperature of the butter.

2. Add the salt and vanilla extract, mixing until combined.

3. Turn the stand mixer off and add dry ingredients. Combine on slow speed until flour is mixed in. This may require turning the mixer off and gathering all the dough by hand, kneading it to combine.

4. Remove the dough from the mixer and place on the counter. Roll the dough into a 10-inch log, about 1 inch in width. Form the dough into a log and roll onto a piece of parchment. Chill the log inside the parchment, placing in the fridge for 30 minutes.

(continued on page 39)

5. While the dough is chilling, preheat the oven to 350°F. Line two cookie trays with parchment paper and set aside.

6. Place raw sugar and reserved vanilla bean pod in a food processor. Pulse together to break up the vanilla bean pod and set aside.

7. Using a pastry brush, brush the outside of the cookie dough log with the beaten egg. Roll the log in the prepared vanilla sugar.

8. Slice the log into ½-inch rounds, and place cookies about 1 inch apart on prepared sheet trays. Bake 9–14 minutes, until cookies are golden brown.

SPRINKLE SOME JOY COOKIES

If you were lucky enough to grow up near a Publix supermarket, this recipe will remind you of a bakery staple: sprinkle sugar cookies. The free bakery cookie was the reason every kid I knew clamored to go to the grocery store. What could be a better complement to produce in your parents' cart but a buttery, sugary sprinkle cookie? Making these at home is the best way to relive the joy of that supermarket stroll—be sure to bake until just golden brown to keep them deliciously soft and chewy.

ACTIVE TIME: 45 minutes | YIELD: Makes 24 cookies
DIFFICULTY: 1 (mixer, cookie scoop)

2½ cups (300 grams) cups all-purpose flour

1 teaspoon (4 grams) baking powder

½ teaspoon (2 grams) kosher salt

2 sticks/1 cup (227 grams) unsalted butter, room temperature

1¼ cups (275 grams) granulated sugar

2 large (100 grams) eggs

2 teaspoons (8 grams) vanilla extract

½ teaspoon (2 grams) almond extract

1 cup (200 grams) rainbow sprinkles

1. Preheat the oven to 350°F. Line two cookie trays with parchment paper and set aside.

2. Whisk together all-purpose flour, baking powder, and salt in a small bowl. Set aside.

3. Using an electric mixer fitted with a paddle attachment, cream together butter and granulated sugar. Mix on medium-high speed until the butter is fluffy and there are no lumps.

4. Once the ingredients are creamed, add the eggs one at a time, mixing until incorporated. Add vanilla and almond extracts and mix until combined.

5. Add dry ingredients and mix until just combined.

6. Using a cookie scoop, portion the cookies and toss into the sprinkles. Place on the prepared trays, spacing the cookies about 3 inches apart.

7. Bake 11–15 minutes, until the centers are cooked through. Allow cookies to cool for at least 5 minutes before removing from sheet trays.

6. Turn the stand mixer off and add dry ingredients. Combine at a slow speed until the mixture is a third of the way combined. Turn the machine off and add chopped chocolate and three-quarters of the crushed potato chips. Mix on slow speed until the mixture just comes together.

7. Portion the cookies using a ¾-ounce cookie scoop. Place on the prepared trays, spacing the cookies about 3 inches apart.

8. Roll cookies in the remaining one-quarter amount of the crushed potato chips.

9. Sprinkle the prepared cookies with Maldon sea salt. Bake until cookies are golden brown, about 12–15 minutes. Allow to cool for at least 5 minutes before removing from the cookie tray.

MONSTER COOKIES

Monster cookies are a mash-up of several crowd-pleasers—M&M's®, oats, chocolate chips, and peanut butter. This is a great cookie for a pantry cleanup. Feel free to "mix it up" using anything you have on hand: Oreo® cookies, white chocolate chips, almond butter—they will all work great!

ACTIVE TIME: 45 minutes | YIELD: Makes 24 cookies
DIFFICULTY: 1 (mixer, cookie scoop)

2½ cups (300 grams) all-purpose flour

2 cups (200 grams) old-fashioned oats

1 teaspoon (4 grams) baking soda

½ teaspoon (2 grams) kosher salt

1 stick/½ cup (113 grams) unsalted butter, room temperature

½ cup (120 grams) creamy peanut butter

1 cup (200 grams) light brown sugar

¼ cup (55 grams) granulated sugar

2 large (100 grams) eggs

2 teaspoons (8 grams) vanilla extract

1 cup (160 grams) M&M's® candies, plus additional (¼ cup/30 grams) to top cookies with

1 cup (170 grams) semisweet chocolate chips

1. Preheat the oven to 350°F. Line two cookie trays with parchment paper and set aside.

2. Whisk together all-purpose flour, old-fashioned oats, baking soda, and salt in a small bowl. Set aside.

3. Using an electric mixer fitted with a paddle attachment, cream together the butter, peanut butter, light brown sugar, and granulated sugar. Mix on medium speed until the butter is fluffy, about 5 minutes.

4. Once the ingredients are creamed, add the eggs one at a time, mixing until incorporated. Add vanilla extract and mix until combined.

5. Add dry ingredients and mix until combined. Add M&M's® candies and chocolate chips and mix until just combined.

6. Portion the cookies using a ¾-ounce cookie scoop. Place on the prepared trays, spacing the cookies about 3 inches apart. Bake 12–15 minutes, until the centers of the cookies are cooked through.

7. Once cookies come out of the oven, top each with an additional 2–3

(continued on next page)

M&M's® candies, gently pushing into the top of each cookie. Allow cookies to cool for at least 5 minutes before removing from the sheet trays.

CHEF'S NOTE: Although I am a fan of making things yourself, store-bought peanut butter is really best for this recipe. In fact, whenever I bake with peanut butter, I recommend using what I call "the good stuff." The plastic jar with the screw cap, sweetened and well emulsified, makes for a good treat. Creamy or extra crunchy both do well in these cookies.

MORNING TREATS

COFFEE CAKE SQUARES

I think the "trick" to high-quality coffee cake is making sure your cake stays incredibly moist and fluffy. I use sour cream, which helps keep the cake tender and adds just the right bit of tang. And yes, it's true—coffee cake contains no actual coffee, but it goes perfectly with a cup of your morning joe.

ACTIVE TIME: 75 minutes | YIELD: Makes 20 two-inch squares
DIFFICULTY: 2 (mixer)

CAKE BATTER

2½ cups (300 grams) all-purpose flour

2 teaspoons (8 grams) baking powder

1 teaspoon (4 grams) baking soda

1 teaspoon (4 grams) kosher salt

1½ sticks/¾ cup (170 grams) unsalted butter, room temperature

1 cup (220 grams) granulated sugar

3 large (150 grams) eggs

1 teaspoon (4 grams) vanilla extract

2 cups (454 grams) sour cream

FILLING

¼ cup (50 grams) light brown sugar

½ teaspoon (2 grams) ground cinnamon

1 cup (125 grams) pecans, chopped

TOPPING

½ cup (100 grams) light brown sugar

1 teaspoon (4 grams) ground cinnamon

¼ cup pecans, (30 grams) chopped

1½ sticks/¾ cup (170 grams) unsalted butter, chilled and cubed

1. Preheat the oven to 350°F. Line a 9-x-13-inch pan with parchment paper and set aside. Be sure to leave overhang on the edges, so you can easily release the bars once they are baked.

2. In a medium bowl, whisk together flour, baking powder, baking soda, and salt. Set aside.

3. Using an electric mixer fitted with a paddle attachment on medium speed, cream together the butter and sugar until well combined and softened, about 3–5 minutes.

4. Reduce the mixer speed to low once the butter and sugar are creamed. Crack eggs into a small bowl, then add eggs and vanilla extract to the mixer. Mix until just combined.

5. Reduce speed to low and add the sour cream, scraping down the bowl and paddle once with a rubber spatula, then mix until combined. Take the bowl off the mixer and fold in the dry ingredients until well combined.

6. Whisk together filling measurements of light brown sugar, ground cinnamon, and chopped pecans in a small bowl. This mixture will be the center of the coffee cake. Set aside until you are ready to assemble.

(continued on next page)

7. Whisk together topping measurements of light brown sugar, ground cinnamon, and chopped pecans in a separate small bowl. Using your hands, pinch the butter-and-light-brown-sugar mixture, continuing until pea-size crumbs form. This will be used for the topping. Set aside.

8. Add half of the coffee cake batter to the cake pan. Top with the filling mixture (step 6). Finish with the remaining half of the cake batter. Top with the streusel topping (step 7). Bake cake for about 35–45 minutes, until it springs back at the touch of your fingertip. Allow the coffee cake to fully cool before slicing into 2-inch squares.

HOMESTYLE CINNAMON ROLLS

There's something about waking up to the smell of cinnamon rolls you intend to share. Cinnamon roll dough is typically made from brioche—a sweetened, enriched bread dough that can be used for so many things. But there is something special about a cinnamon roll. I love the art in this process. It starts with prepping the brioche dough. But then you stop to rest before the second proof. The next morning, you wake up to bring the dough to room temperature and wait for them to proof before putting them in the oven. It's a labor of love and a perfect treat to share with the ones you love. Bonus: Your home will smell incredible!

ACTIVE TIME: 90 minutes | DOWN TIME: Overnight rest
YIELD: Makes 12 cinnamon rolls | DIFFICULTY: 3 (mixer, offset spatula, rolling pin)

BRIOCHE DOUGH

1 cup (245 grams) whole milk

2¼ teaspoons (8 grams) instant yeast

3 large (150 grams) eggs

4½ cups (500 grams) all-purpose flour

¼ cup (55 grams) granulated sugar

1 teaspoon (4 grams) kosher salt

1 stick/½ cup (113 grams) unsalted butter, cubed

CINNAMON FILLING

¾ stick/6 tablespoons (85 grams) unsalted butter, softened

1 cup (200 grams) light brown sugar

¼ cup (80 grams) maple syrup

2 teaspoons (8 grams) ground cinnamon

¼ teaspoon (1 gram) kosher salt

CREAM CHEESE TOPPING

1 block/8 ounces (224 grams) cream cheese, room temperature

2 tablespoons (24 grams) whole milk

1 teaspoon (4 grams) vanilla extract

½ teaspoon (2 grams) kosher salt

1 cup (120 grams) confectioners' sugar

1. Begin by preparing the dough. Pour milk into the bowl of a standing mixer fitted with a dough hook. Pour in yeast and whisk by hand to combine. Whisk in eggs.

2. Add the all-purpose flour, granulated sugar, and kosher salt to the bowl. Mix dough together on slow speed for about 3 minutes. The dough should begin to come together.

3. While the machine is mixing, add butter in pieces to the dough. Once all the butter has been added, turn

(continued on page 53)

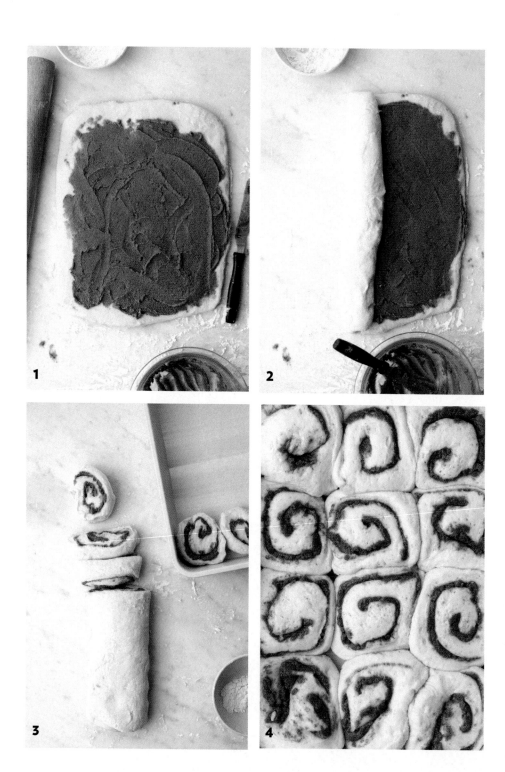

the machine to medium speed and allow to mix for about 8–12 minutes. When the dough is finished, it should pass these three steps: wrap around the hook, come away from the bowl cleanly, and create the windowpane effect, described on page 20.

4. Place the dough in a bowl and cover with plastic wrap or a kitchen towel. Allow to double in size (about 40 minutes) at room temperature. Once doubled, tightly wrap the bowl in plastic wrap and store in the refrigerator for at least 4 hours, or overnight.

ASSEMBLING THE ROLLS

1. Using a medium bowl, combine all filling ingredients. Using a rubber spatula, beat together until a smooth paste is formed. Set aside.

2. Line a 9-x-13-inch pan with parchment paper and set aside.

3. Lightly flour your work surface. Using a rolling pin, roll brioche dough into a thin rectangle, about 12 inches long and 8 inches wide.

4. Spread the cinnamon filling all over the dough. Beginning at the side closest to you, roll the dough into a log.

5. Place the rolled log onto a cutting board. Using a sharp knife, slice into ½-inch pieces, about 12 rolls total. Place in the prepared baking pan.

6. Cover the rolls loosely with plastic wrap and allow them to double in size, about 40 minutes. While the rolls proof, begin preparing the topping and preheat the oven to 350°F.

7. Place cream cheese in a stand mixer fitted with a paddle attachment. Beat until smooth. Add remaining ingredients and mix. Taste and adjust the consistency by adding more sugar or milk, as needed. The topping should be thick, but spreadable at room temperature.

8. Check that proofing buns have doubled in size and are warm to the touch. Bake for 25 minutes, or until the cinnamon buns are golden brown and reach an internal temperature of 190°F. Allow rolls to cool for about 5 minutes before spreading cream cheese frosting on top.

LEMON BREAKFAST CAKE

Once this cake is fully cool, I like to place it in the refrigerator for at least 12 hours before slicing it. I find giving the cake an overnight rest gives it the best crumb structure and the yogurt keeps the cake deliciously moist. Serve this cake with some fresh berries and whipped cream for a morning treat!

ACTIVE TIME: 75 minutes | **YIELD:** 1 loaf, approximately 8 slices
DIFFICULTY: 1

---

1 cup (120 grams) all-purpose flour

½ cup (45 grams) almond flour

2 teaspoons (8 grams) baking powder

¼ teaspoon (1 gram) kosher salt

1 cup (220 grams) granulated sugar

½ cup (125 grams) plain yogurt

3 large (150 grams) eggs

1 teaspoon (4 grams) vanilla extract

½ teaspoon (2 grams) lemon extract

½ cup (110 grams) canola oil

Zest of 1 lemon

1. Preheat the oven to 350°F. Line a loaf pan with parchment paper and spray with nonstick spray. Set aside.

2. Whisk together all-purpose flour, almond flour, baking powder, and salt in a medium bowl. Set aside.

3. Whisk together sugar, yogurt, eggs, vanilla extract, lemon extract, canola oil, and lemon zest in a large bowl until well combined.

4. Using a rubber spatula, fold dry ingredients into wet until just combined. Add cake batter to the prepared loaf pan and smooth for an even top.

5. Bake until cake springs back to the touch and is golden brown, about 45 minutes. Cool before releasing from the pan. Allow lemon breakfast cake to fully cool before slicing into eight 1-inch pieces.

CHOCOLATE SWIRL BABKA

I like to think of babka as a Jewish cinnamon bun. It's not something I grew up eating, but once I discovered it in New York City, I had to learn how to make it. I like mine with chocolate filling, but cinnamon is also a popular option. You want to be careful to bake this until it's just done, keeping the middle gooey and soft.

ACTIVE TIME: 90 minutes | DOWN TIME: Overnight rest

YIELD: Makes 2 loaves, about 12 pieces | DIFFICULTY: 3 (mixer, offset spatula)

BRIOCHE DOUGH

1 cup (245 grams) whole milk

2¼ teaspoons (8 grams) instant yeast

3 large (150 grams) eggs

4½ cups (500 grams) all-purpose flour

¼ cup (55 grams) granulated sugar

1 teaspoon (4 grams) kosher salt

1 stick/½ cup (113 grams) unsalted butter, cubed

BABKA FILLING

½ stick/4 tablespoons (56 grams) unsalted butter, cubed

1 cup (170 grams) dark chocolate, chopped and divided in half

2 tablespoons (28 grams) unsweetened cocoa powder

2 tablespoons (28 grams) granulated sugar

½ teaspoon (2 grams) kosher salt

STREUSEL TOPPING

⅓ cup (40 grams) all-purpose flour

2 tablespoons (28 grams) granulated sugar

2 teaspoons (5 grams) unsweetened cocoa powder

¼ teaspoon (1 gram) kosher salt

¼ stick/2 tablespoons (28 grams) unsalted butter, melted

SIMPLE SYRUP FOR FINISHING

2 tablespoons (28 grams) granulated sugar

2 tablespoons (30 grams) hot water, for simple syrup

---

1. Pour milk into the bowl of a stand mixer fitted with a dough hook. Pour in yeast and whisk by hand to combine. Whisk in eggs.

2. Add the all-purpose flour, granulated sugar, and kosher salt to the bowl. Mix dough together on slow speed, for about 3 minutes. The dough should begin to come together.

3. With the machine running, add butter in pieces to the dough. Once all the butter has been added, turn the machine to a medium speed and allow to mix for about 8–12 minutes. When the dough is finished, it should pass these three steps: wrap around the hook, come away from the bowl cleanly, and create the windowpane effect, described on page 20.

(continued on next page)

4. Place the dough in a bowl and cover with plastic wrap or a kitchen towel. Allow to double in size (about 40 minutes) at room temperature. Once doubled, tightly wrap the bowl in plastic wrap and store in the refrigerator for at least 4 hours or overnight.

ASSEMBLING THE BABKA

1. Before beginning assembly, prepare the filling and streusel.

2. Combine the butter, ½ cup of the dark chocolate, cocoa powder, granulated sugar, and salt in a small pot. Melt over low heat to combine, making a spread. Allow the mixture to cool before you assemble the loaf. Set aside remaining ½ cup chopped dark chocolate for assembly.

3. In a small bowl, add the flour, sugar, cocoa powder, and salt. Pour melted butter over the dry ingredients and toss together. Set aside for assembly.

4. Line two loaf pans with parchment paper and spray with nonstick spray. Set aside.

5. Divide rested babka dough in half, keeping the second half of the dough covered. Lightly flour a surface, and using a rolling pin, roll into a rectangle 10 inches by 8 inches.

6. Spread chocolate mixture evenly over rolled-out dough. Sprinkle half of the chopped chocolate (about ¼ cup) on the top. The beginning of this procedure is similar to steps 3 and 4 in the assembly of the cinnamon rolls on pages 51 and 52.

7. Beginning at the side closest to you, roll the dough into a log. Gently press to seal.

8. Roll top and tuck under and keep rolling. Seal at end. Elongate slightly to make sure the roll is even but try not to stretch the dough. Cut the log in half lengthwise to create two logs. Pinch the top of both ends together and twist two logs together. Place in a loaf pan, cover, and allow to proof. Repeat with the second half of the dough.

9. Once proofed, top with streusel and bake at 350°F for about 35–45 minutes, until golden brown and the internal temperature reaches at least 190°F. While the babka is baking, whisk together the granulated sugar and hot water to prepare your simple syrup. Before babka is fully cooled, use a pastry brush and finish the babka with simple syrup.

SEA SALT BUTTERMILK BISCUITS

I have been making these biscuits for many years. They can be used for anything from strawberry shortcakes to chicken sandwiches. When I was working at Aspen Kitchen in Colorado, I started my mornings with scrambled eggs and a biscuit left over from dinner service the night before. I highly recommend it. These also go great with the homemade jam from the Lemon Raspberry Cupcakes on page 83.

ACTIVE TIME: 45 minutes | YIELD: 8 biscuits
DIFFICULTY: 1 (round cutters)

---

2 cups (240 grams) all-purpose flour

2 teaspoons (8 grams) baking powder

½ teaspoon (2 grams) baking soda

1 teaspoon (4 grams) kosher salt

2 teaspoons (8 grams) granulated sugar

1 stick/½ cup (113 grams) unsalted butter, cubed and chilled

1 cup (225 grams) buttermilk, plus extra for brushing biscuit tops

Maldon sea salt (coarse sea salt), as needed for garnish

1. Preheat the oven to 400°F. Line a cookie sheet tray with a piece of parchment paper and set aside.

2. Place flour, baking powder, baking soda, salt, and sugar in a bowl and whisk together.

3. Using your hands, rub the butter into the flour mixture, continuing until walnut-size pieces form.

4. Make a well in the flour mixture and add the buttermilk, mixing until a dough comes together.

5. Turn the dough out onto a lightly floured surface and use a rolling pin to roll the dough to 1 inch in height.

6. Using a 2-inch round cutter, punch out biscuit circles. Place each biscuit round on the prepared sheet tray. Reroll remaining dough up to two more times, punching out additional biscuits.

7. Using a pastry brush, lightly brush each biscuit round with buttermilk. Sprinkle with Maldon sea salt to taste.

8. Bake biscuits for 15–18 minutes, until golden brown. Allow biscuits to cool for at least 5 minutes before removing from the sheet tray.

QUARANTINE BANANA BREAD

When COVID-19 started, banana bread and sourdough filled our daily discussions as much as vaccinations and testing swabs. It seemed that everyone was baking. I have always loved banana bread, especially with chocolate. Whenever possible, I love to use my favorite, Valrhona Caramelia milk chocolate. I love sneaking it into this banana bread for a special treat. If you are able to find Valrhona Caramelia, try chopping it into bite-size pieces and using it instead of the chocolate chips for a caramel banana bread treat.

ACTIVE TIME: 75 minutes | YIELD: 1 loaf, approximately 8 slices
DIFFICULTY: 2

1½ cups (180 grams) all-purpose flour

1 teaspoon (4 grams) baking soda

1 teaspoon (4 grams) kosher salt

1 stick/½ cup (113 grams) unsalted butter, room temperature

2 tablespoons (25 grams) canola oil

1 cup (210 grams) granulated sugar

2 large (100 grams) eggs

1 teaspoon (4 grams) vanilla extract

3 ripe (360 grams) bananas, mashed

1 cup (170 grams) milk chocolate chips (or chopped milk chocolate, such as Valrhona Caramelia 36%)

Turbinado sugar, as needed for garnish

---

1. Preheat the oven to 350°F. Line a loaf pan with parchment paper and spray with nonstick spray. Set aside.

2. Whisk together all-purpose flour, baking soda, and salt in a medium bowl. Set aside.

3. Place butter in a medium saucepan over medium-high heat. Gently swirl the butter, allowing it to melt evenly. Once the butter is melted, continue to heat until it is a medium amber color. Set aside to cool for about 5–8 minutes. Butter should not be warm, but not cool to the touch.

4. In a medium bowl, whisk together browned butter, canola oil, and granulated sugar until well combined. Add eggs and vanilla extract and mix thoroughly.

5. Using a rubber spatula, fold the mashed bananas into the mixture. Add dry ingredients and mix until combined. Fold in chocolate chips or chopped milk chocolate.

6. Place batter into prepared loaf pan. Sprinkle raw sugar on the top.

7. Bake until golden brown and the center comes out clean with a toothpick, about 45–55 minutes. Allow banana bread to fully cool before slicing into eight 1-inch pieces.

BARS AND BITES

MY DAD'S FAVORITE BROWNIES

These brownies bring back great memories. I was inspired by a recipe for White Chocolate Brownies with Macadamia Nuts in the cookbook *Chocolate*, by Christine McFadden and Christine France. My mom is a lifelong bookworm, and we picked up the cookbook on one of her many, many bookstore trips. To say they became a staple in my house would be an understatement. They were my dad's favorite dessert, and I made them whenever I could. In the midst of the COVID-19 crisis, I experienced the third anniversary of my dad's passing. I made my revised version in his honor, complete with a special delivery to the Physical Therapy Department at NYU Hospital. I promised I would honor his legacy through "everything chocolate," and these brownies are a big part of that story.

ACTIVE TIME: 45 minutes | YIELD: 12 brownies

DIFFICULTY: 2 (offset spatula)

---

1 cup (120 grams) all-purpose flour

½ teaspoon (2 grams) baking powder

½ (2 grams) teaspoon kosher salt

1 cup/6 ounces (170 grams) white chocolate, chopped

1 stick/½ cup (113 grams) unsalted butter, cubed

½ cup (110 grams) granulated sugar

2 large (100 grams) eggs

1 teaspoon (4 grams) vanilla extract

¾ cup (120 grams) semisweet chocolate chips

1 cup/6 ounces (170 grams) milk chocolate, chopped

1½ cups (185 grams) unsalted macadamia nuts, chopped

1. Preheat the oven to 350°F. Line a 9-inch cake pan with parchment paper and set aside.

2. Whisk together all-purpose flour, baking powder, and kosher salt in a medium bowl and set aside.

3. Using a small saucepan over low heat, melt white chocolate, butter, and granulated sugar. Continuously mix, using a rubber spatula, making sure the mixture doesn't burn. Once the mixture has melted, set it aside to cool.

4. Once cooled to room temperature, whisk in the eggs and vanilla extract. Switch back to the rubber spatula, and fold in the dry ingredients until just combined. Add the chocolate chips, gently stirring so they do not melt. Pour into the prepared pan and use an offset spatula to spread the mixture out evenly.

(continued on next page)

5. Bake 25–30 minutes, until golden brown and a cake tester comes out clean. While the brownies bake, begin melting the milk chocolate in a double boiler or in the microwave (see page 20 for chocolate melting instructions).

6. Remove brownies from the oven and pour melted chocolate over the top, spreading evenly into a thin layer. Top with chopped macadamia nuts, gently pushing down to make sure they stick. Allow brownies to fully cool before slicing into 1-inch wedges.

SUGAR COOKIE BITES

Everything about these bars is a party! Because they are quite sweet, I like to cut them into bite-size portions so they're not too overwhelming. Try not to overbake these, as you want them light and chewy. Make sure you allow them to fully cool before adding your frosting. I like to slice them once the frosting sets up in the refrigerator, using a hot knife to get clean cuts, then serve them at room temperature.

ACTIVE TIME: 60 minutes | **DOWN TIME:** 30 minutes

YIELD: About 48 bite-size bars | **DIFFICULTY: 1**

COOKIES

2½ cups (275 grams) cake flour

1 teaspoon (4 grams) baking powder

½ teaspoon (2 grams) kosher salt

2 sticks/1 cup (227 grams) unsalted butter, room temperature

1 cup/8 ounces (224 grams) cream cheese, room temperature

1½ cups (315 grams) granulated sugar

2 large (100 grams) eggs

2 teaspoons (8 grams) vanilla extract

2 teaspoons (10 grams) rainbow sprinkles

FROSTING

American buttercream (recipe on page 18)

1. Preheat the oven to 350°F. Line a 9-x-13-inch pan with parchment paper and set aside. Be sure to leave overhang on the edges so the bars can easily be removed once baked.

2. Place cake flour, baking powder, and kosher salt in a bowl. Whisk together and set aside.

3. Using an electric mixer fitted with a paddle attachment, cream together butter and cream cheese on medium speed until well combined and softened, about 3-5 minutes.

4. Add granulated sugar and mix until combined.

5. Add eggs and vanilla, mixing until combined.

6. Add the flour and mix until just combined. Using a rubber spatula, fold in rainbow sprinkles.

7. Spread mixture onto prepared pan, making sure it is evenly distributed. Bake in a preheated oven for about 20–25 minutes, until it is just light golden brown. Remove from the oven and allow the bars to fully cool down. While they cool, prepare frosting.

(continued on page 71)

8. Using an electric mixer fitted with a paddle attachment on medium speed, beat butter until it becomes fluffy and just off-white.

9. Add confectioners' sugar and mix until well combined. Add heavy cream, vanilla extract, and salt. Mix until well combined. Add 1–2 drops of gel food dye, mixing until it reaches the desired color.

10. Spread frosting on top of the baked cookie layer. Garnish with sprinkles. Allow to set up in the refrigerator before slicing into bite-size bars.

BROWN BUTTER M&M'S® BARS

Using brown butter in these simple bars takes these treats to the next level. Feel free to customize this recipe with M&M's® of your choice—Holiday-Themed, Peanut, or even Pretzel M&M's® would be great.

ACTIVE TIME: 60 minutes | YIELD: About 20 two-inch brownies
DIFFICULTY: 1

---

2 cups (240 grams) all-purpose flour

1 teaspoon (4 grams) baking soda

1 teaspoon (4 grams) kosher salt

2 sticks/1 cup (224 grams) unsalted butter

1 cup (210 grams) granulated sugar

¾ cup (150 grams) light brown sugar

3 large (150 grams) eggs

1 tablespoon (12 grams) vanilla extract

1½ cups (260 grams) semisweet chocolate chips

1 cup (160 grams) M&M's®, plus additional (¼ cup/30 grams) for topping

1. Preheat the oven to 350°F. Line a 9-x-13-inch pan with parchment paper and set aside. Leave overhang on the edges, so you can easily release the bars once they are baked.

2. In a small bowl, whisk together all-purpose flour, baking soda, and salt. Set aside.

3. Place butter in a medium saucepan over medium-high heat. Gently swirl the butter, allowing it to melt evenly. Once the butter is melted, continue to cook until the butter is a medium amber color. Set aside to cool for about 5–8 minutes. Butter should not be warm, but not cool to the touch.

4. Pour browned butter into a medium bowl. Whisk in granulated sugar and light brown sugar. Add eggs and vanilla extract, whisking well.

5. Using a rubber spatula, fold in dry ingredients and mix until just combined. Add the chocolate chips and M&M's®.

6. Transfer the bar mixture to the prepared pan, using a spatula to spread the mixture out evenly.

7. Bake for 25–35 minutes, until the edges are just golden brown. Remove from the oven and immediately add remaining M&M's® on top of the bars, for garnish. Allow bars to fully cool before slicing.

AMPED-UP RICE KRISPIES TREATS™

When I started #BakeItForward, the movement grew so fast, I couldn't keep up. Suddenly I had a calendar full of deliveries, and all the cookie scooping and baking was becoming very time-consuming! A friend suggested a simple classic: Rice Krispies Treats™. I like to add Oreo® cookies to mine, but you can add chocolate chips, peanut butter cups, or sprinkles for a fun twist.

ACTIVE TIME: 20 minutes | YIELD: About 24 one-inch squares
DIFFICULTY: 1

---

12 chocolate sandwich cookies (like Oreo®)

½ stick/4 tablespoons (56 grams) unsalted butter

1-pound bag (454 grams) mini marshmallows

5 cups (125 grams) puffed rice cereal

1 cup (170 grams) white chocolate chips

1. Grease a 9-x-13-inch baking pan with nonstick spray. Place sandwich cookies in a ziptop bag and, using a rolling pin, crush into chunks.

2. Over medium heat, melt butter in a large pot. I like to get mine a little bit past melted and just beginning to brown.

3. Add marshmallows and stir over low heat until marshmallows are melted.

4. Add remaining ingredients and toss well to combine. Pour into the prepared baking pan and use a spatula to spread the mixture out evenly.

5. Allow to cool completely. Remove from the pan and slice into 24 squares.

CITRUS SHORTBREAD SQUARES

Something about citrus desserts will always remind me of growing up in Florida, where we had a lime tree in our backyard. I helped my dad pick fresh limes for our Sunday barbecues. Those limes made their way into many of our family meals, and this shortbread is no exception. These squares will transport you to a place where the warm breeze blows through the palm trees and the salt air tastes like home.

ACTIVE TIME: 45 minutes | **DOWN TIME:** 60 minutes
YIELD: About 12 two-inch squares | **DIFFICULTY:** 2

SHORTBREAD CRUST

1 cup (120 grams) all-purpose flour

¼ teaspoon (1 gram) kosher salt

¼ cup (55 grams) granulated sugar

1 teaspoon (4 grams) vanilla extract

1 stick/½ cup (113 grams) unsalted butter

CITRUS FILLING

1 cup (220 grams) granulated sugar

3 tablespoons (36 grams) all-purpose flour

3 large (150 grams) eggs

½ cup (115 grams) lemon, lime, or blood orange juice

Powdered sugar, for garnish

1. Preheat oven to 350°F. Line an 8-inch-square baking pan with parchment paper and set aside. Be sure to leave overhang on the edges so the bars can be easily removed once baked.

2. Melt butter in a small saucepan. Set aside.

3. Whisk together all-purpose flour, kosher salt, and granulated sugar in a medium bowl.

4. Stir in vanilla extract and melted butter, using a rubber spatula.

5. Pour shortbread mixture into the prepared baking tray. Use hands to press down, making an even base. Bake until a light golden brown, about 15 minutes. Remove from the oven.

6. Prepare the citrus filling while the shortbread is baking. Sift together granulated sugar and all-purpose flour.

7. Whisk together eggs and citrus juice in a small bowl. Whisk eggs and citrus juice into sifted sugar and flour to combine all the filling ingredients.

(continued on next page)

8. Pour over warm shortbread, place in the oven, and continue baking, about 20–25 minutes, until filling is set. It will be just golden brown on the outside and should appear firm on the top.

9. Allow to cool to room temperature before placing in the refrigerator. Chill for at least 1–2 hours before slicing. For best slicing, use a warm knife, cleaning between cuts. Dust with powdered sugar before serving.

CHEF'S NOTE: Fresh juice truly makes a world of difference, so take the time to squeeze some yourself. You won't regret it. I know you may be tempted to buy pre-squeezed citrus juice, but using fresh will make these citrus squares bright and flavorful.

LITTLE CELEBRATIONS

MINI COOKIE CAKES

Before cookie cakes really came into style, bakeries used to sell mini cookie cups that were garnished with frosting and a candy topper. They were my favorite treat, and these are an ode to them. At my neighborhood mall growing up, my parents picked me up right by a Mrs. Fields® cookie bakery. These cookies are like a flashback to my childhood in every bite.

ACTIVE TIME: 75 minutes | YIELD: About 28 mini cookie cakes

DIFFICULTY: 2 (mixer, mini cupcake tin, pastry bag)

COOKIE DOUGH

1 cup (120 grams) all-purpose flour

½ teaspoon (2 grams) baking soda

¼ teaspoon (1 gram) kosher salt

¾ stick/6 tablespoons (85 grams) unsalted butter, room temperature

¼ cup (55 grams) granulated sugar

⅓ cup (65 grams) light brown sugar

1 large (50 grams) egg

1 teaspoon (4 grams) vanilla extract

1 cup (170 grams) chocolate chips

2 tablespoons (28 grams) rainbow sprinkles

FROSTING

1 stick/½ cup (113 grams) unsalted butter, room temperature

1½ cups (180 grams) confectioners' sugar, sifted

2 teaspoons (8 grams) heavy cream

1 teaspoon (4 grams) vanilla extract

½ teaspoon (2 grams) kosher salt

Gel food dye (optional)

1. Preheat the oven to 350°F. Line a mini muffin tray with cupcake liners or grease pan with nonstick spray. Set aside.

2. Whisk together all-purpose flour, baking soda, and salt in a small bowl. Set aside.

3. Using an electric mixer fitted with a paddle attachment on medium speed, cream together butter, granulated sugar, and brown sugar. Mix on medium-high speed until the butter is fluffy and there are no lumps, about 3–5 minutes.

4. Once the ingredients are creamed, pour the egg into the creamed butter, mixing until well combined. Add vanilla extract and mix until combined.

5. Add dry ingredients and mix until just combined. Remove the bowl from the mixer, and, using a rubber spatula, fold in chocolate chips and sprinkles, mixing until just combined.

6. Portion cookie dough into small balls and fill the mini muffin molds about two-thirds of the way up.

(continued on next page)

7. Bake 12–15 minutes, until the centers are cooked through. Allow cookies to cool before frosting.

8. While cookies are cooling, prepare the frosting. Using an electric mixer fitted with a paddle attachment on medium speed, beat butter until it becomes fluffy and just off-white, about 5 minutes.

9. Add confectioners' sugar and mix until well combined. Add heavy cream, vanilla extract, and salt. Mix again until well combined. Add 1 or 2 drops of gel food dye, mixing until the frosting reaches desired color.

10. Using a pastry bag, pipe swirls onto each cooled cookie. Garnish with sprinkles, if desired.

CHEF'S NOTE: If you don't have a mini cupcake tin, feel free to adapt this recipe as you see fit. You can make the cookie dough in a cake pan and make a family style cookie cake, or use regular-size muffin tins for a larger treat.

LEMON RASPBERRY CUPCAKES

Using freeze-dried fruit in frosting is one of my absolute favorite pastry chef tricks. The fruit gives this frosting a dainty pale pink color without adding any food dye. When you use freeze-dried fruit all the moisture has been removed, so you can get a burst of flavor without changing the consistency of your buttercream.

ACTIVE TIME: 75 minutes | YIELD: 12 cupcakes
DIFFICULTY: 2 (mixer, mini cupcake tin)

CUPCAKE BATTER

1¼ cup (150 grams) all-purpose flour

1½ teaspoons (6 grams) baking powder

½ teaspoon (2 grams) kosher salt

1 lemon, zested

½ cup (110 grams) canola oil

¾ cup (170 grams) granulated sugar

3 large (150 grams) eggs

1 teaspoon (4 grams) vanilla extract

½ teaspoon (2 grams) lemon extract

¼ cup (60 grams) whole milk

¼ cup (60 grams) plain yogurt or sour cream

RASPBERRY JAM

2 cups (250 grams) fresh or frozen raspberries

¾ cup (170 grams) plus 2 tablespoons (24 grams) granulated sugar

1 lemon, zested and juiced

1 tablespoon (12 grams) fruit pectin

AMERICAN BUTTERCREAM FROSTING

(procedure on page 18)

2 sticks/1 cup (225 grams) unsalted butter, room temperature

3 cups (360 grams) confectioners' sugar, sifted

1 tablespoon (12 grams) heavy cream

1 teaspoon (4 grams) vanilla extract

½ teaspoon (2 grams) kosher salt

½ cup (35 grams) freeze-dried raspberries, crushed

Lemon zest and fresh raspberries, for garnish

---

1. Preheat the oven to 350°F. Using cupcake liners, line a 12-cup muffin pan and set aside.

2. Whisk together flour, baking powder, salt, and lemon zest in a small bowl.

3. Whisk together oil and sugar in a medium bowl. Add eggs, vanilla extract, and lemon extract. Mix until well combined. Add milk and yogurt/sour cream, mixing again until well combined.

(continued on page 85)

4. Fold dry ingredients into wet, using a rubber spatula until just combined.

5. Portion the cake batter into prepared tins, filling about three-quarters of the way up.

6. Bake cupcakes for about 18–24 minutes, until they are golden brown and spring back at the touch of a fingertip. Allow to cool before filling and frosting.

7. While cupcakes cool, prepare raspberry jam for inside of cupcakes. Place raspberries, ¾ cup granulated sugar, and lemon zest and juice in a medium-size pot.

8. Using a rubber spatula, stir together, making sure nothing is sticking to the bottom. Over medium-high heat bring the mixture to a boil, continually stirring. Allow mixture to boil for about 3 minutes.

9. Whisk together remaining 2 tablespoons granulated sugar with the fruit pectin. Add the mixture to the boiling fruit and stir to fully combine. Bring back to a boil for 3 more minutes, allowing jam to thicken.

10. Take jam off the heat and fully cool down before using.

11. While the jam is cooling, prepare the frosting. In a stand mixer fitted with a paddle, cream the butter, about 8 minutes, until it is light, fluffy, and almost white in color.

12. Turn the mixer off and add the confectioners' sugar. Slowly increase speed and continue beating until it is combined and fluffy in texture. Add heavy cream and mix. Add vanilla extract and kosher salt and mix until fully combined. Add the crushed freeze-dried raspberries. Taste and adjust raspberry flavor or salt, as needed. Transfer to a pastry bag fitted with a pastry tip.

13. Using an apple corer or a small knife, remove the center of each cupcake, keeping the bottom of the cupcake intact. Fill each cupcake with cooled raspberry jam. Frost each cupcake with frosting and add fresh raspberries. Garnish with additional lemon zest.

HOSTESS WITH THE MOSTEST CAKES

I hope these little chocolatey bites remind you of a very well-known grocery store cupcake. I'd like to think these are every bit as indulgent with just a little bit of effort. Moist chocolate cake, marshmallow filling, and dark chocolate ganache. It makes me nostalgic for my childhood.

ACTIVE TIME: 90 minutes | **YIELD:** About 12 cupcakes
DIFFICULTY: 3 (mixer, pastry bag)

CUPCAKES

1 cup (115 grams) all-purpose flour

1 teaspoon (4 grams) baking soda

½ teaspoon (2 grams) kosher salt

½ cup (55 grams) unsweetened cocoa powder

½ stick (57 grams) unsalted butter, melted

1 cup (220 grams) granulated sugar

2 large (100 grams) eggs

1 teaspoon (4 grams) vanilla extract

¼ cup (65 grams) whole milk

½ cup (120 grams) brewed coffee

MARSHMALLOW CREAM FILLING

3 large (90 grams) egg whites

½ cup (110 grams) granulated sugar

¼ teaspoon (1 gram) kosher salt

½ teaspoon (2 grams) vanilla extract

CHOCOLATE GANACHE

1¼ cups (175 grams) dark chocolate

¼ cup plus 2 tablespoons (88 grams) heavy cream

1 tablespoon (12 grams) light corn syrup

1 tablespoon (14 grams) unsalted butter

1. Preheat the oven to 350°F. Line a 12-cup muffin tin with cupcake liners and set aside.

2. Whisk together all-purpose flour, baking soda, salt, and cocoa powder in a small bowl.

3. Whisk together melted butter and sugar in a medium bowl. Whisk in eggs and vanilla extract.

4. Whisk in whole milk and coffee until well combined.

5. Fold dry ingredients into wet using a rubber spatula, until just combined.

6. Using a scoop, portion the cake batter into prepared muffin tins, filling about three-quarters of the way to the top.

(continued on next page)

7. Bake cupcakes for about 18–24 minutes, until golden brown and the cake springs back to the touch. Allow to cool before filling and frosting.

8. Prepare marshmallow cream filling. Fill a medium-size pot with water about one-third of the way and bring to a boil. Set the bowl from the stand mixer on top of the pot, creating a double boiler.

9. Add egg whites, sugar, and salt to the bowl and whisk together. Keep whisking until the internal temperature of the egg white mixture reaches 160°F, checking with an instant read thermometer. The sugar should be completely dissolved, and the mixture should be warm.

10. Place the bowl with the egg white mixture back onto the stand mixer fitted with a whisk attachment. Turn mixer on high speed, whipping egg whites until the mixture cools down, approximately 6 minutes. Add vanilla extract and whisk until combined.

11. Place three-quarters of the marshmallow cream in a pastry bag fitted with a ¼-inch round tip, and the remaining marshmallow cream in a pastry bag fitted with a smaller, 1/8-inch round tip. Set aside both bags of marshmallow cream for assembly.

12. Prepare ganache. Use the same pot of water, refilling to one-third of the way full if necessary. Bring the water to a simmer.

13. Carefully melt the chocolate over the simmering water, stirring until the chocolate is completely melted. Set aside.

14. In a small pot, bring cream and light corn syrup to a boil. Once the mixture comes to a boil, gently pour over the melted chocolate.

15. Add the butter and stir with a rubber spatula until the ganache appears smooth, shiny, and elastic. Set aside for assembly.

ASSEMBLY

1. Using a paring knife, poke a hole into the top of each cupcake. Using the pastry bag with the larger, ¼-inch round tip, pipe the marshmallow frosting into each cupcake, filling until the cupcake begins to feel heavy but not overflowing.

2. Dip each filled cupcake in ganache, covering the top of the cupcake. Set aside and allow ganache to set.

3. Use the remaining pastry bag of marshmallow cream (with the smaller, 1/8-inch round tip) to decorate the top of each cupcake with swirls.

NYC-STYLE CHALLAH

I love challah. I could eat it every day. This beautiful centerpiece bread is perfect for all to enjoy and doubles as the best French toast the next morning. I like to add everything bagel seasoning to the top of mine, but you may garnish as you like.

ACTIVE TIME: 75 minutes | DOWN TIME: 2 hours
YIELD: 1 loaf | DIFFICULTY: 2 (mixer)

¾ cup (175 grams) water, room temperature

2 teaspoons (7 grams) instant yeast

2 large (100 grams) eggs

2 tablespoons (30 grams) canola oil

3 cups (450 grams) all-purpose flour

3 tablespoons (30 grams) granulated sugar

2 teaspoons (8 grams) kosher salt

1 egg mixed with 1 teaspoon water (for egg wash)

3 tablespoons (30 grams) everything bagel seasoning (see note on page 18)

1. Combine water and yeast in a medium bowl, whisking until yeast is dissolved. Add eggs and oil, whisking until combined. Add all-purpose flour, granulated sugar, and kosher salt and mix until well combined using a rubber spatula.

2. Mix together until ingredients begin to form a loose, shaggy dough. Move dough to the table and begin to knead. Knead dough for about 6–10 minutes, until it forms a smooth ball.

3. Place in an oiled bowl and cover with plastic wrap. Allow dough to rise for about 1 hour, or until it doubles in size.

4. Divide dough into 3 equal pieces. Roll dough into logs. Each log should be slightly thicker in the middle and thinner on the ends. Braid the pieces, layering each log on top of the other, and tuck the ends under the assembled loaf.

5. Gently egg wash dough; cover with plastic wrap and allow to proof about 45 minutes. Preheat the oven to 350°F.

6. Once the dough has proofed and grown in size to be nearly doubled, repeat the egg wash and garnish with everything bagel seasoning. Bake at 350°F for 30–40 minutes, or until golden brown. Allow to cool completely before slicing and serving.

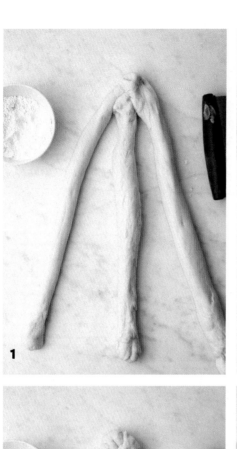

STRAWBERRY HAND PIES

Hand pies are the perfect on-the-go treat, and I love how cute and inviting these are. Make sure your ingredients for your pie dough are cold to ensure it's easy to work with (warm ingredients would make your dough a sticky mess).

ACTIVE TIME: 90 minutes | DOWN TIME: 2 hours | YIELD: 6 hand pies
DIFFICULTY: 3 (rolling pin, round cutters, pastry bag)

PIE DOUGH

1¾ cup (225 grams) all-purpose flour

1½ teaspoons (6 grams) granulated sugar

1 teaspoon (4 grams) kosher salt

1 stick/½ cup, plus 2 tablespoons (125 grams) cold, unsalted butter, cubed

½ cup (85 grams) ice-cold water, plus more if needed

STRAWBERRY FILLING

2 cups (320 grams) strawberries, trimmed

2 tablespoons (24 grams) granulated sugar

2 teaspoons (6 grams) cornstarch

Zest and juice of 1 lime

HAND PIE ASSEMBLY

1 egg mixed with 1 teaspoon water (for egg wash)

Granulated sugar, as needed, to sprinkle on top

1. Whisk the flour, sugar, and salt together in a large mixing bowl to combine.

2. Rub the butter into the dry ingredients by hand and mix until butter is reduced to small pieces about the size of a pea.

3. Slowly add about half of the ice-cold water. Using a rubber spatula (or your hands), begin to bring the dough together. Adjust the water as needed to achieve the right consistency. When a handful of dough can be squeezed together and holds its shape, the dough has enough water added to it. There will be lumps of butter remaining in the dough, and the dough should just begin to hold together. If it is sticky, add a small amount of flour. If it is too dry, add a small amount of water.

4. Wrap pie dough tightly in plastic wrap and refrigerate until firm, 1 to 2 hours. The dough can also rest in the refrigerator overnight.

5. Prepare strawberry filling while the pie dough is chilling. Combine all ingredients in a small pot and cook over medium heat until the strawberries begin to break down and the mixture begins to thicken, about 8 minutes.

6. Place strawberry filling in a bowl and set aside to fully cool. Line a cookie tray with parchment paper and set aside.

(continued on next page)

7. Once strawberry filling is no longer warm, begin to roll out your pie dough. Lightly flour work surface. Using a rolling pin, roll pie dough until it is about ⅛ inch thick. Using a 4-inch round cutter, cut out rounds. Place on a prepared cookie tray.

8. Using a pastry brush, create a border of egg wash on half of the rounds. Spoon strawberry filling into the center and top with the second half of the rounds. Pinch the outside, releasing any air bubbles. Using a fork, crimp the edges. Using a paring knife, cut an X in the center of each pie. Place each pie on the prepared sheet tray.

9. Brush the top of the hand pies with egg wash and sprinkle with sugar. Bake at 375°F for about 20–30 minutes, until golden brown and the fruit is bubbling. Allow to cool for at least 5 minutes before removing from the sheet tray.

CLASSIC YEAST DOUGHNUTS

People always ask me what my favorite doughnut shop is, and honestly, I don't have an answer. What I can say is that doughnuts are a process of love and they've become a form of meditation for me. This classic, pure doughnut—my plain-Jane glazed—is the best place to start. To me, it's the true test of a high-quality doughnut.

ACTIVE TIME: 120 minutes | **DOWN TIME:** Overnight (ideal) or 6-hour rest
YIELD: About 12 doughnuts | **DIFFICULTY:** 3 (rolling pin, round cutters)

DOUGHNUT DOUGH

2 tablespoons (30 grams) water, room temperature

2¼ teaspoons (8 grams) instant yeast

6 large (300 grams) eggs

4¼ cups (510 grams) high-gluten flour

¼ cup (55 grams) granulated sugar

2 teaspoons (8 grams) kosher salt

2 sticks/1 cup (224 grams) butter, cold and cubed

Canola oil, as needed to deep-fry doughnuts

VANILLA GLAZE

3½ cups (454 grams) confectioners' sugar

¼ cup (75 grams) milk

1 teaspoon (4 grams) vanilla extract

½ teaspoon (2 grams) kosher salt

1. Pour water into the bowl of a standing mixer fitted with a dough hook. Add yeast and whisk by hand to combine. Whisk in eggs.

2. Add the high-gluten flour, granulated sugar, and kosher salt to the bowl. Mix dough together on slow speed for about 3 minutes until it begins to come together.

3. Add butter in pieces to the dough while the machine is still running. Once all the butter has been added, turn the machine to medium speed and allow to mix for about 8–12 minutes. When the dough is finished, it should pass these three steps: wrap around the hook, come away from the bowl cleanly, and create the windowpane effect, described on page 20.

4. Place the dough in a bowl and cover with plastic wrap or a kitchen towel. Allow to double in size (about 40 minutes) at room temperature. Once doubled, tightly wrap the bowl in plastic wrap and store in the refrigerator for at least 6 hours or overnight.

(continued on page 97)

Once doughnut dough has rested, prepare to roll and punch out doughnut shapes.

5. Lightly sprinkle flour onto a cookie tray and set aside. Lightly flour work surface. Using a rolling pin, roll dough to ½-inch thickness and using a doughnut cutter, portion into doughnut shapes. Place doughnuts on the prepared cookie tray, leaving space for them to grow. Cover with plastic wrap or a kitchen towel and proof at room temperature until they double in size, approximately 1 hour.

6. Prepare vanilla glaze while doughnuts are proofing. Whisk together confectioners' sugar, milk, vanilla extract, and salt. Adjust consistency as needed; add more milk for a thinner glaze or additional confectioners' sugar for a thicker glaze.

7. Preheat frying oil to 360°F on the stovetop using a large pot or, alternatively, a tabletop fryer. Line a sheet pan with a rack or paper towels. Doughnuts are ready for the fryer once they have doubled in size and are warm to the touch.

8. Lightly flour your fingertips and gently place 3 to 4 doughnuts in the hot fryer oil. Fry until golden brown, about 90 seconds on each side. Remove from the fryer using a slotted spoon or spider strainer. Drain and cool on the rack or paper-towel–lined sheet tray. Once cool to the touch, dip each doughnut in the vanilla glaze and allow glaze to drip down the sides. Allow doughnuts to cool slightly before serving.

COMMUNITY THANKS

#BakeItForward started with one batch of cookies. But before long, the movement had raised enough money to purchase enough ingredients for me to bake every day for nearly three months (!) to thank those on the front lines. I received generous product donations and many, many Venmo transfers. As a community we raised money for not just #BakeItForward, but also for City Harvest, in a generous donation. To think that this project has now resulted in a cookbook gives me pause, for it wouldn't be possible without an entire community's effort. They say it takes a village, and for that I am forever grateful.

Every recipe in this book was tested, first by me and then by my friends, family, and even some strangers thanks to the magic of the internet. The recipes are provided in both grams and volume, so you can use whichever you are most comfortable with. Thank you to every person who tested these recipes. Your energy allowed me to make this cookbook a reality.

Michael, Claire, and Bo Franey
Chelsea Claire
Ananya Modi
Rachel and Mike MacDonald
Michelle Schmidt
Rikita Peebles
Kim Rojas
Jen Jacobs
Tracy Zimmermann
Lauren Trakhman
Alex Cauley
Jamie Saltzman
Madeline Malloy
Samantha Friedman
Dustin and Dylan Deville
Mallory Kojkowski
Meredith Brooks
Marla Bowman
Kelley Baxter
Christine Rahilly
Sara Tane
Rochelle, Hank, Conner, and
    Logan Newman
Kyle Trobman

Brie Krug
Daisy Mendez
Aleksandra Alfonso
Dave, Liz, and Vaida Lieberman
Lauren Anderson
Danielle Sunseri
Gerard Pietrafesa Jr.
Katy Mora
Katrina Barrios
Alyssa Sadoff
Linda Katz Brandt
Barney Agate
Nicole Kaufman Black, Hailey
    Claus-Allen, and Ny'vaeh
    Sims-Colebrook
Amanda Danforth
Jamie Forester
Linda Ogden
Eric Norton
Ed Knapp
Sarah Bergman
Carly Norton
Debbie Pease
Francesca Giannettino

ACKNOWLEDGMENTS

A few weeks after graduating college, I picked up my life and moved to New York City to begin my journey of becoming a pastry chef. I didn't have a plan when I started, but my friends and family stood behind me the whole way through. I am the luckiest.

To my friends who have cheered me on since the very beginning, and to those who made this book a reality:

Katy, Katrina, Ashley, Maria, Ruby: You are my constant eating partners, forever sisters, and stellar taste-testers. We can always blame Katy for helping me take the plunge to go to culinary school, but I guess she was right. Special thanks to Maria for her art direction and careful placement of the sprinkles, as demonstrated on the cover art.

Janie: Thank you for being my quarantine friend, co-chef, and creative backbone.

Michelle: Your kindness reminds me how far being kind can go. You are my personal health hero.

Sara: Building this with you is a highlight of my life. You pushed me, and you are a part of this story. Ellory and Emerson: You are my greatest joys.

Morgan: Thank you for designing our very first logo and allowing your art to shine on many cookie boxes.

Marla: Thank you for being my on-call lawyer and always having my back. I promise to always be your on-call pastry chef.

Alex: I am so grateful we were able to work on this project together. Thank you for such beautiful photos and allowing me to cover your home in sprinkles.

Hadley: I hope working on this book is just the beginning of your pastry career. I cannot wait to watch how baby rhino grows.

Sandra: I truly lucked out when my newest coworker also became my editor. I look forward to a future of many more sweet projects together.

I would be nothing without my family. Rachel, thank you for being my sounding board, my cheerleader, and my ultimate taste-tester. Mike, I promise to always include chocolate chip cookies as a part of our dessert spreads. Mom, everything I am is because of you. Knowing you are all in my life means we can do anything. I hope to continue to be in charge of the desserts (and all of the food) for every family gathering forever.

And to every student I have met in person and virtually over the years—thank you for helping me find myself. Teaching you has taught me more than I thought possible.

INDEX